# Treatise on Faith and the Creed

# Treatise on Faith and the Creed

St. Augustine

# Treatise on Faith and the Creed



Written by: St. Augustine (Nov.13 354 – Aug.28 430)

Translated by: Rev. S.D.F Salmond, D.D (1838 – 1905)

Updated into Modern U.S English by A.M. Overett (b. 1960)



Published by
Lighthouse Christian Publishing
SAN 257-4330
5531 Dufferin Drive
Savage, Minnesota, 55378
United States of America

www.lighthousechristianpublishing.com

## Introductory Notice.

The occasion and date of the composition of this treatise are indicated in a statement which Augustin makes in the seventeenth chapter of the First Book of his Retractations.

From this we learn that, in its original form, it was a discourse which Augustin, when only a presbyter, was requested to deliver in public by the bishops assembled at the Council of Hippo-Regius, and that it was subsequently issued as a book at the desire of friends. The general assembly of the North African Church, which was thus convened at what is now Bona, in the modern territory of Algiers, took place in the year 393 A.D., and was otherwise one of some historical importance, on account of the determined protest which it emitted against the position elsewhere allowed to Patriarchs in the Church, and against the admittance of any more authoritative or magisterial title to the highest ecclesiastical official than that of simply "Bishop of the first Church" (primæ sedis episcopus).

The work constitutes an exposition of the several clauses of the so-called Apostles' Creed. The questions concerning the mutual relations of the three Persons in the Godhead are handled with greatest fullness; in connection with which, especially in the use made of the analogies of Being, Knowledge, and Love, and in the cautions thrown in against certain applications of these and other illustrations taken from things of human experience, we come across sentiments which are also repeated in the City of God, the books on the Trinity, and others of his doctrinal writings.

The passage referred to in the Retractations is as follows: About the same period, in presence of the bishops, who gave me orders to that effect, and who were holding a plenary Council of the whole of Africa at Hippo-Regius, I delivered, as presbyter, a discussion on the subject of Faith and the Creed. This disputation, at the very pressing request of some of those who were on terms of more than usual intimacy and affection with us, I threw into the form of a book, in which the themes themselves are made the subjects of discourse, although not in a method involving the adoption of the particular connection of words which is given to the competentes to be committed to memory. In this book, when discussing the question of the resurrection of the flesh, I say: 'Rise again the body will, according to the Christian faith, which is incapable of deceiving. And if this appears incredible to anyone, [it is because] he looks simply to what the flesh is at present, while he fails to consider of what nature it shall be hereafter. For at that time of angelic change it will no more be flesh and blood, but only body;' and so on, through the other statements which I have made there about the change of bodies terrestrial into bodies celestial, as the apostle, when he spoke from the same point, said, 'Flesh and blood shall not inherit the kingdom of God.' But if any one takes these declarations in a sense leading him to suppose that the earthly body, such as we now have it, is changed in the resurrection into a celestial body, in any such wise as that neither these members nor the substance of the flesh will subsist any more, undoubtedly he must be set right, by being put in mind of the body of the Lord, who subsequently to His resurrection appeared in the same members, as One who was not only to be seen with the eyes, but also handled with the hands; and made His possession of the flesh likewise surer by the discourse which He spoke, saying, 'Handle me, and see; for a spirit hath not flesh and bones, as ye see me have.' Hence it is certain that the apostle did not deny that the substance of the flesh will exist in the kingdom of God, but that under the name of 'flesh and blood' he designated either men who live after the flesh, or the express corruption of the flesh, which assuredly at that period shall subsist no more. For after he had said, 'Flesh and blood shall not inherit the kingdom of God,' what he proceeds to say next, —namely, 'neither shall corruption inherit incorruption,'—is rightly taken to have been added by way of explaining his previous statement. And on this subject, which is one on which it is difficult to convince unbelievers, anyone who reads my last book, On the City of God, will find that I have discoursed with the utmost carefulness of which I am capable. The performance in question commences thus: 'Since it is written,' etc."

## Chapter 1. —Of the Origin and Object of the Composition.

1. Inasmuch as it is a position, written and established on the most solid foundation of apostolic teaching, "that the just lives of faith;" and inasmuch also as this faith demands of us the duty at once of heart and tongue, —for an apostle says, "With the heart man believeth unto righteousness, and with the mouth confession is made unto salvation,"—it becomes us to be mindful both of righteousness and of salvation. For, destined as we are to reign hereafter in everlasting righteousness, we certainly cannot secure our salvation from the present evil world, unless at the same time, while laboring for the salvation of our neighbors, we likewise with the mouth make our own profession of the faith which we carry in our heart. And it must be our aim, by pious and careful watchfulness, to provide against the possibility of the said faith sustaining any injury in us, on any side, through the fraudulent artifices [or, cunning fraud] of the heretics.

We have, however, the catholic faith in the Creed, known to the faithful and committed to memory, contained in a form of expression as concise as has been rendered admissible by the circumstances of the case; the purpose of which [compilation] was, that individuals who are but beginners and sucklings among those who have been born again in Christ, and who have not yet been strengthened by most diligent and spiritual handling and understanding of the divine Scriptures, should be furnished with a summary, expressed in few words, of those matters of necessary belief which were subsequently to be explained to them in many words, as they made progress and rose to [the height of] divine doctrine, on the assured and steadfast basis of humility and charity. It is underneath these few words, therefore, which are thus set in order in the Creed, that most heretics have endeavored to conceal their poisons; whom divine mercy has withstood, and still withstands, by the instrumentality of spiritual men, who have been counted worthy not only to accept and believe the catholic faith as expounded in those terms, but also thoroughly to understand and apprehend it by the enlightenment imparted by the Lord. For it is written, "Unless ye believe, ye shall not understand." But the handling of the faith is of service for the protection of the Creed; not, however, to the intent that this should itself be given instead of the Creed, to be committed to memory and repeated by those who are receiving the grace of God, but that it may guard the matters which are retained in the Creed against the insidious assaults of the heretics, by means of catholic authority and a more entrenched defense.

## Chapter 2. —Of God and His Exclusive Eternity.

2. For certain parties have attempted to gain acceptance for the opinion that God the Father is not Almighty: not that they have been bold enough expressly to affirm this, but in their traditions they are convicted of entertaining and crediting such a notion. For when they affirm that there is a nature which God Almighty did not create, but of which at the same time He fashioned this world, which they admit having been disposed in beauty, they thereby deny that God is almighty, to the effect of not believing that He could have created the world without employing, for the purpose of its construction, another nature, which had been in existence previously, and which He Himself had not made. Thus, forsooth, [they reason] from their carnal familiarity with the sight of craftsmen and house-builders, and artisans of all descriptions, who have no power to make good the effect of their own art unless they get the help of materials already prepared. And so these parties in like manner understand the Maker of the world not to be almighty, if thus He could not fashion the said world without the help of some other nature, not framed by Himself, which He had to use as His materials. Or if indeed they do allow God, the Maker of the world, to be almighty, it becomes matter of course that they must also acknowledge that He made out of nothing the things which He did make. For, granting that He is almighty, there cannot exist

anything of which He should not be the Creator. For although He made something out of something, as man out of clay, nevertheless He certainly did not make any object out of aught which He Himself had not made; for the earth from which the clay comes He had made out of nothing. And even if He had made out of some material the heavens and the earth themselves, that is to say, the universe and all things which are in it, according as it is written, "Thou who didst make the world out of matter unseen," or also "without form," as some copies give it; yet we are under no manner of necessity to believe that this very material of which the universe was made, although it might be "without form," although it might be "unseen," whatever might be the mode of its subsistence, could possibly have subsisted of itself, as if it were co-eternal and co-eval with God. But whatsoever that mode was which it possessed to the effect of subsisting in some manner, whatever that manner might be, and of can take on the forms of distinct things, this it did not possess except by the hand of Almighty God, by whose goodness it is that everything exists, —not only every object which is already formed, but also every object which is formable. This, moreover, is the difference between the formed and the formable, that the formed has already taken on form, while the formable can take the same. But the same Being who imparts form to objects, also imparts the capability of being formed. For of Him and in Him is the fairest figure of all things, unchangeable; and therefore He Himself is One, who communicates to everything its possibilities, not only that it be beautiful actually, but also that it be capable of being beautiful. For which reason we do most right to believe that God made all things of nothing. For, even although the world was made of some sort of material, this self-same material itself was made of nothing; so that, in accordance with the most orderly gift of God, there was to enter first the capacity of taking forms, and then that all things should be formed which have been formed. This, however, we have said, in order that no one might suppose that the utterances of the divine Scriptures are contrary the one to the other, in so far as it is written at once that God made all things of nothing, and that the world was made of matter without form.

3. As we believe, therefore, in God the Father Almighty, we ought to uphold the opinion that there is no creature which has not been created by the Almighty. And since He created all things by the Word, which Word is also designated the Truth, and the Power, and the Wisdom of God, —as also under many other appellations the Lord Jesus Christ, who is commended to our faith, is presented likewise to our mental apprehensions, to wit, our Deliverer and Ruler, the Son of God; for that Word, by whose means all things were founded, could not have been begotten by any other than by Him who founded all things by His instrumentality; —

## Chapter 3. —Of the Son of God, and His Peculiar Designation as the Word.

—Since this is the case, I repeat, we believe also in Jesus Christ, the Son of God the Only-Begotten of the Father, that is to say, His Only Son, our Lord. This Word however, we ought not to apprehend merely in the sense in which we think of our own words, which are given forth by the voice and the mouth, and strike the air and pass on, and subsist no longer than their sound continues. For that Word remains unchangeably: for of this very Word was it spoken when of Wisdom it was said, "Remaining in herself, she makes all things new." Moreover, the reason of His being named the Word of the Father, is that the Father is made known by Him. Accordingly, just as it is our intention, when we speak truth, that by means of our words our mind should be made known to him who hears us, and that whatever we carry in secrecy in our heart may be set forth by means of signs of this sort for the intelligent understanding of another individual; so this Wisdom that God the Father begot is most appropriately named His Word, inasmuch as the most hidden Father is made known to worthy minds by the same.

4. Now there is a very great difference between our mind and those words of ours, by which we endeavor to set

forth the said mind. We indeed do not beget intelligible words, but we form them; and in the forming of them the body is the underlying material. Between mind and body, however, there is the greatest difference. But God, when He begot the Word, begot that which He is Himself. Neither out of nothing, nor of any material already made and founded did He then beget; but He begot of Himself that which He is Himself. For we too aim at this when we speak, (as we shall see) if we carefully consider the inclination of our will; not when we lie, but when we speak the truth. For to what else do we direct our efforts then, but to bring our own very mind, if it can be done at all, in upon the mind of the hearer, with the view of its being apprehended and thoroughly discerned by him; so that we may indeed abide in our very selves, and make no retreat from ourselves, and yet at the same time put forth a sign of such a nature as that by it a knowledge of us may be effected in another individual; that thus, so far as the faculty is granted us, another mind may be, as it were, put forth by the mind, whereby it may disclose itself? This we do, making the attempt both by words, and by the simple sound of the voice, and by the countenance, and by the gestures of the body, —by so many contrivances, in sooth, desiring to make patent that which is within; inasmuch as we are not able to put forth aught of this nature [in itself completely]: and thus it is that the mind of the speaker cannot become perfectly known; thus also it results that a place is open for falsehoods. God the Father, on the other hand, who possessed both the will and the power to declare Himself with the utmost truth to minds designed to obtain knowledge of Him, with the purpose of thus declaring Himself begot this [Word] which He Himself is who did beget; which [Person] is likewise called His Power and Wisdom, inasmuch as it is by Him that He has wrought all things, and in order disposed them; of whom these words are for this reason spoken: "She (Wisdom) reaches from one end to another mightily, and sweetly doth she order all things."

Chapter 4. —Of the Son of God as Neither Made by the Father nor Less Than the Father, and of His Incarnation.

5. Wherefore The Only-Begotten Son of God was neither made by the Father; for, according to the word of an evangelist, "all things were made by Him:" nor begotten instantaneously; since God, who is eternally wise, has with Himself His eternal Wisdom: nor unequal with the Father, that is to say, in anything less than He; for an apostle also speaks in this wise, "Who, although He was constituted in the form of God, thought it not robbery to be equal with God." By this catholic faith, therefore, those are excluded, on the one hand, who affirm that the Son is the same [Person] as the Father; for [it is clear that] this Word could not possibly be with God, were it not with God the Father, and [it is just as evident that] He who is alone is equal to no one. And, on the other hand, those are equally excluded who affirm that the Son is a creature, although not such an one as the rest of the creatures are. For however great they declare the creature to be, if it is a creature, it has been fashioned and made. For the terms fashion and create mean one and the same thing; although in the usage of the Latin tongue the phrase create is employed at times instead of what would be the strictly accurate word beget. But the Greek language makes a distinction. For we call that creatura (creature) which they call κτίσμαοr κτίσις; and when we desire to speak without ambiguity, we use not the word creare (create), but the word condere (fashion, found). Consequently, if the Son is a creature, however great that may be, He has been made. But we believe in Him by whom all things (omnia) were made, not in Him by whom the rest of things (cetera) were made. For here again we cannot take this term all things in any other sense than as meaning whatsoever things have been made.

6. But as "the Word was made flesh, and dwelt among us," the same Wisdom which was begotten of God condescended also to be created among men. There is a reference to this in the word, "The Lord created me in the beginning of His ways." For the beginning of His ways is the

Head of the Church, which is Christ endued with human nature (homine indutus), by whom it was purposed that there should be given to us a pattern of living, that is, a sure way by which we might reach God. For by no other path was it possible for us to return but by humility, who fell by pride, according as it was said to our first creation, "Taste, and ye shall be as gods." Of this humility, therefore, that is to say, of the way by which it was needful for us to return, our Restorer Himself has deemed it meet to exhibit an example in His own person, "who thought it not robbery to be equal with God, but emptied Himself, taking the form of a servant;" in order that He might be created Man in the beginning of His ways, the Word by whom all things were made. Wherefore, in so far as He is the Only-begotten, He has no brethren; but in so far as He is the First-begotten, He has deemed it worthy of Him to give the name of brethren to all those who, subsequently to and by means of His pre-eminence, are born again into the grace of God through the adoption of sons, according to the truth commended to us by apostolic teaching. Thus, then, the Son according to nature (naturalis filius) was born of the very substance of the Father, the only one so born, subsisting as that which the Father is, God of God, Light of Light. We, on the other hand, are not the light by nature, but are enlightened by that Light, so that we may be able to shine in wisdom. For, as one says, "that was the true Light, which lightest every man that cometh into the world." Therefore we add to the faith of things eternal likewise the temporal dispensation of our Lord, which He deemed it worthy of Him to bear for us and to minister in behalf of our salvation. For in so far as He is the only-begotten Son of God, it cannot be said of Him that He was and that He shall be, but only that He is; because, on the one hand, that which was, now is not; and, on the other, that which shall be, as yet is not. He, then, is unchangeable, independent of the condition of times and variation. And it is my opinion that this is the very consideration to which was due the circumstance that He introduced to the apprehension of His servant Moses the kind of name [which He then adopted]. For when he asked of Him by whom he should say that he was sent, in the event of the people to whom he was being sent despising him, he received his answer when He spoke in this wise: "I Am that I Am." Thereafter, too, He added this: "Thus shalt thou say unto the children of Israel, He that is (Qui est) has sent me unto you."

7. From this, I trust, it is now made patent to spiritual minds that there cannot possibly exist any nature contrary to God. For if He is, —and this is a word which can be spoken with propriety only of God (for that which truly is remains unchangeably; inasmuch as that which is changed has been something which now it is not, and shall be something which as yet it is not), —it follows that God has nothing contrary to Himself. For if the question were put to us, What is contrary to white? we would reply, black; if the question were, What is contrary to hot? we would reply, cold; if the question were, What is contrary to quick? we would reply, slow; and all similar interrogations we would answer in like manner. When, however, it is asked, What is contrary to that which is? the right reply to give is, that which is not.

8. But whereas, in a temporal dispensation, as I have said, with a view to our salvation and restoration, and with the goodness of God acting therein, our changeable nature has been assumed by that unchangeable Wisdom of God, we add the faith in temporal things which have been done with salutary effect on our behalf, believing in that Son of God Who Was Born Through the Holy Ghost of the Virgin Mary. For by the gift of God, that is, by the Holy Spirit, there was granted to us so great humility on the part of so great a God, that He deemed it worthy of Him to assume the entire nature of man (totum hominem) in the womb of the Virgin, inhabiting the material body so that it sustained no detriment (integrum), and leaving it without detriment. This temporal dispensation is in many ways craftily assailed by the heretics. But if anyone shall have grasped the catholic faith, so as to believe that the entire nature of man was assumed by the Word of God, that is to say, body, soul, and spirit, he has sufficient defense against those parties. For surely, since that assumption was effected in behalf of our

salvation, one must be on his guard lest, as he believes that there is something belonging to our nature which sustains no relation to that assumption, this something may fail also to sustain any relation to the salvation. And seeing that, with the exception of the form of the members, which has been imparted to the varieties of living objects with differences adapted to their different kinds, man is in nothing separated from the cattle but in [the possession of] a rational spirit (rationali spiritu), which is also named mind (mens), how is that faith sound, according to which the belief is maintained, that the Wisdom of God assumed that part of us which we hold in common with the cattle, while He did not assume that which is brightly illumined by the light of wisdom, and which is man's peculiar gift?

9. Moreover, those parties also are to be abhorred who deny that our Lord Jesus Christ had in Mary a mother upon earth; while that dispensation has honored both sexes, at once the male and the female, and has made it plain that not only that sex which He assumed pertains to God's care, but also that sex by which He did assume this other, in that He bore [the nature of] the man (virum gerendo), [and] in that He was born of the woman. Neither is there anything to compel us to a denial of the mother of the Lord, in the circumstance that this word was spoken by Him: "Woman, what have I to do with thee? Mine hour is not yet come." But He rather admonishes us to understand that, in respect of His being God, there was no mother for Him, the part of whose personal majesty (cujus majestatis personam) He was preparing to show forth in the turning of water into wine. But about His being crucified, He was crucified in respect of his being man; and that was the hour which had not come as yet, at the time when this word was spoken, "What have I to do with thee? Mine hour is not yet come;" that is, the hour at which I shall recognize thee. For at that period, when He was crucified as man, He recognized His human mother (hominem matrem), and committed her most humanely (humanissime) to the care of the best beloved disciple. Nor, again, should we be moved by the fact that, when the presence of His mother and His brethren was announced to

Him, He replied, "Who is my mother, or who my brethren?" etc. But rather let it teach us, that when parents hinder our ministry wherein we minister the word of God to our brethren, they ought not to be recognized by us. For if, on the ground of His having said, "Who is my mother?" everyone should conclude that He had no mother on earth, then each should as matter of course be also compelled to deny that the apostles had fathers on earth; since He gave them an injunction in these terms: "Call no man your father upon the earth; for one is your Father, which is in heaven."

10. Neither should the thought of the woman's womb impair this faith in us, to the effect that there should appear to be any necessity for rejecting such a generation of our Lord for the mere reason that worthless men consider it unworthy (sordidi sordidam putant). For most true are these sayings of an apostle, both that "the foolishness of God is wiser than men," and that "to the pure all things are pure." Those, therefore, who entertain this opinion ought to ponder the fact that the rays of this sun, which indeed they do not praise as a creature of God, but adore as God, are diffused all the world over, through the noisomenesses of sewers and every kind of horrible thing, and that they operate in these according to their nature, and yet never become debased by any defilement thence contracted, albeit that the visible light is by nature in closer conjunction with visible pollutions. How much less, therefore, could the Word of God, who is neither corporeal nor visible, sustain defilement from the female body, wherein He assumed human flesh together with soul and spirit, through the incoming of which the majesty of the Word dwells in a less immediate conjunction with the frailty of a human body! Hence it is manifest that the Word of God could in no way have been defiled by a human body, by which even the human soul is not defiled. For not when it rules the body and quickens it, but only when it lusts after the mortal good things thereof, is the soul defiled by the body. But if these persons were to desire to avoid the defilements of the soul, they would dread rather these falsehoods and profanities.

## Chapter 5. —Of Christ's Passion, Burial, and Resurrection.

11. But little [comparatively] was the humiliation (humilitas) of our Lord on our behalf in His being born: it was also added that He deemed it meet to die in behalf of mortal men. For "He humbled Himself, being made subject even unto death, yea, the death of the cross:" lest anyone of us, even were he able to have no fear of death [in general], should yet shudder at some particular sort of death which men reckon most shameful. Therefore do we believe in Him Who Under Pontius Pilate Was Crucified and Buried. For it was requisite that the name of the judge should be added, with a view to the cognizance of the times. Moreover, when that burial is made an object of belief, there enters also the recollection of the new tomb, which was meant to present a testimony to Him in His destiny to rise again to newness of life, even as the Virgin's womb did the same to Him in His appointment to be born. For just as in that sepulcher no other dead person was buried, whether before or after Him; so neither in that womb, whether before or after, was anything mortal conceived.

12. We believe also, that On the Third Day He Rose Again from The Dead, the first begotten for brethren destined to come after Him, whom He has called into the adoption of the sons of God, whom [also] He has deemed it meet to make His own joint-partners and joint-heirs.

## Chapter 6. —Of Christ's Ascension into Heaven.

13. We believe that He Ascended into Heaven, which place of blessedness He has likewise promised unto us, saying, "They shall be as the angels in the heavens," in that city which is the mother of us all, the Jerusalem eternal in the heavens. But it is wanting to give offense to certain parties, either impious Gentiles or heretics, that we should believe in the assumption of an earthly body into heaven. The Gentiles, however, for the most part, set themselves diligently to ply us with the arguments of the philosophers,

to the effect of affirming that there cannot possibly be anything earthly in heaven. For they know not our Scriptures, neither do they understand how it has been said, “It is sown an animal body, it is raised a spiritual body.” For thus it has not been expressed, as if body were turned into spirit and became spirit; inasmuch as at present, too, our body, which is called animal (animale), has not been turned into soul and become soul (anima). But by a spiritual body is meant one which has been made subject to spirit in such wise that it is adapted to a heavenly habitation, all frailty and every earthly blemish having been changed and converted into heavenly purity and stability. This is the change concerning which the apostle likewise speaks thus: “We shall all rise, but we shall not all be changed.” And that this change is made not unto the worse, but unto the better, the same [apostle] teaches, when he says, “And we shall be changed.” But the question as to where and in what manner the Lord’s body is in heaven, is one which it would be altogether over-curious and superfluous to prosecute. Only we must believe that it is in heaven. For it pertains not to our frailty to investigate the secret things of heaven, but it does pertain to our faith to hold elevated and honorable sentiments on the subject of the dignity of the Lord’s body.

Chapter 7. —Of Christ’s Session at the Father’s Right Hand.

14. We believe also that He Sits at the Right Hand of the Father. This, however, is not to lead us to suppose that God the Father is, as it were, circumscribed by a human form, so that, when we think of Him, a right side or a left should suggest itself to the mind. Nor, again, when it is thus said in express terms that the Father sits, are we to fancy that this is done with bended knees; lest we should fall into that profanity, in [dealing with] which an apostle execrates those who “changed the glory of the incorruptible God into the likeness of corruptible man.” For it is unlawful for a Christian to set up any such image for God in a temple; much more nefarious is it, [therefore], to set it up in the

heart, in which truly is the temple of God, provided it be purged of earthly lust and error. This expression, “at the right hand,” therefore, we must understand to signify a position in supremest blessedness, where righteousness and peace and joy are; just as the kids are set on the left hand, that is to say, in misery, by reason of unrighteousness, labors, and torments. And in accordance with this, when it is said that God “sits,” the expression indicates not a posture of the members, but a judicial power, which that Majesty never fails to possess, as He is always awarding deserts as men deserve them (digna dignis tribuendo); although at the last judgment the unquestionable brightness of the only-begotten Son of God, the Judge of the living and the dead, is destined yet to be a thing much more manifest among men.

## Chapter 8. —Of Christ’s Coming to Judgment.

15. We believe also, that at the most seasonable time He Will Come from Thence, and Will Judge the Quick and the Dead: whether by these terms are signified the righteous and sinners, or whether it be the case that those persons are here called the quick, whom at that period He shall find, previous to [their] death, upon the earth, while the dead denote those who shall rise again at His advent. This temporal dispensation not only is, as holds good of that generation which respects His being God, but also hath been and shall be. For our Lord hath been upon the earth, and at present He is in heaven, and [hereafter] He shall be in His brightness as the Judge of the quick and the dead. For He shall yet come, even so as He has ascended, according to the authority which is contained in the Acts of the Apostles. It is in accordance with this temporal dispensation, therefore, that He speaks in the Apocalypse, where it is written in this wise: “These things says He, who is, and who was, and who is to come.”

Chapter 9. —Of the Holy Spirit and the Mystery of the Trinity.

16. The divine generation, therefore, of our Lord, and his human dispensation, having both been thus systematically disposed and commended to faith, there is added to our Confession, with a view to the perfecting of the faith which we have regarding God, [the doctrine of] The Holy Spirit, who is not of a nature inferior to the Father and the Son, but, so to say, consubstantial and co-eternal: for this Trinity is one God, not to the effect that the Father is the same [Person] as the Son and the Holy Spirit, but to the effect that the Father is the Father, and the Son is the Son, and the Holy Spirit is the Holy Spirit; and this Trinity is one God, according as it is written, "Hear, O Israel, the Lord your God is one God." At the same time, if we be interrogated about each separately, and if the question be put to us, "Is the Father God?" we shall reply, "He is God." If it be asked whether the Son is God, we shall answer to the same effect. Nor, if this kind of inquiry be addressed to us with respect to the Holy Spirit, ought we to affirm in reply that He is anything else than God; being earnestly on our guard, [however], against an acceptance of this merely in the sense in which it is applied to men, when it is said, "Ye are gods." For of all those who have been made and fashioned of the Father, through the Son, by the gift of the Holy Spirit, none are gods according to nature. For it is this same Trinity that is signified when an apostle says, "For of Him, and in Him, and through Him, are all things." Consequently, although, when we are interrogated about each [of these Persons] severally, we reply that that particular one regarding whom the question is asked, whether it be the Father, or the Son, or the Holy Spirit, is God, no one, notwithstanding this, should suppose that three Gods are worshipped by us.

17. Neither is it strange that these things are said about an ineffable Nature, when even in those objects which we discern with the bodily eyes, and judge of by the bodily sense, something similar holds good. For take the instance

of an interrogation about a fountain, and consider how we are unable then to affirm that the said fountain is itself the river; and how, when we are asked about the river, we are as little able to call it the fountain; and, again, how we are equally unable to designate the draught, which comes of the fountain or the river, either river or fountain. Nevertheless, in the case of this trinity we use the name water [for the whole]; and when the question is put regarding each of these separately, we reply in each several instances that the thing is water. For if I inquire whether it is water in the fountain, the reply is given that it is water; and if we ask whether it is water in the river, no different response is returned; and in the case of the said draught, no other answer can possibly be made: and yet, for all this, we do not speak of these things as three waters, but as one water. At the same time, of course, care must be taken that no one should conceive of the ineffable substance of that Majesty merely as he might think of this visible and material fountain, or river, or draught. For in the case of these latter that water which is at present in the fountain goes forth into the river, and does not abide in itself; and when it passes from the river or from the fountain into the draught, it does not continue permanently there where it is taken from. Therefore it is possible here that the same water may be in view at one time under the appellation of the fountain and at another under that of the river, and at a third under that of the draught. But in the case of that Trinity, we have affirmed it to be impossible that the Father should be sometime the Son, and sometime the Holy Spirit: just as, in a tree, the root is nothing else than the root, and the trunk (robur) is nothing else than the trunk, and we cannot call the branches anything else than branches; for, what is called the root cannot be called trunk and branches; and the wood which belongs to the root cannot by any sort of transference be now in the root, and again in the trunk, and yet again in the branches, but only in the root; since this rule of designation stands fast, so that the root is wood, and the trunk is wood, and the branches are wood, while nevertheless it is not three woods that are thus spoken of, but only one. Or, if these objects have some sort of dissimilarity, so that on account of their difference in strength they may be spoken of, without any absurdity, as three woods; at least all parties admit the force of the former example, —namely, that if three cups be filled out of one fountain, they may certainly be called three cups, but cannot be spoken of as three waters, but only as one altogether. Yet, at the same time, when asked concerning the several cups, one by one, we may answer that in each of them by itself there is water; although in this case no such transference takes place as we were speaking of as occurring from the fountain into the river. But these examples in things material (corporalia exempla) have been adduced not in virtue of their likeness to that divine Nature, but in reference to the oneness which subsists even in things visible, so that it may be understood to be quite a possibility for three objects of some sort, not only severally, but also all together, to obtain one single name; and that in this way no one may wonder and think it absurd that we should call the Father God, the Son God, the Holy Spirit God, and that nevertheless we should say that there are not three Gods in that Trinity, but one God and one substance.

18. And, indeed, on this subject of the Father and the Son, learned and spiritual men have conducted discussions in many books, in which, so far as men could do with men, they have endeavored to introduce an intelligible account as to how the Father was not one personally with the Son, and yet the two were one substantially; and as to what the Father was individually (proprie), and what the Son: to wit, that the former was the Begetter, the latter the Begotten; the former not of the Son, the latter of the Father: the former the Beginning of the latter, whence also He is called the Head of Christ, although Christ likewise is the Beginning, but not of the Father; the latter, moreover, the Image of the former, although in no respect dissimilar, and although absolutely and without difference equal (omnino et indifferenter æqualis). These questions are handled with greater breadth by those who, in less narrow limits than ours are at present, seek to set forth the profession of the Christian faith in its totality. Accordingly, in so far as He is the Son, of the Father

received He it that He is, while that other [the Father] received not this of the Son; and in so far as He, in unutterable mercy, in a temporal dispensation took upon Himself the [nature of] man (hominem),—to wit, the changeable creature that was thereby to be changed into something better,—many statements concerning Him are discovered in the Scriptures, which are so expressed as to have given occasion to error in the impious intellects of heretics, with whom the desire to teach takes precedence of that to understand, so that they have supposed Him to be neither equal with the Father nor of the same substance. Such statements [are meant] as the following: "For the Father is greater than I;" and, "The head of the woman is the man, the Head of the man is Christ, and the Head of Christ is God;" and, "Then shall He Himself be subject unto Him that put all things under Him;" and, "I go to my Father and your Father, my God and your God," together with some others of like tenor. Now all these have had a place given them, [certainly] not with the object of signifying an inequality of nature and substance; for to take them so would be to falsify a different class of statements, such as, "I and my Father are one" (unum); and, "He that hath seen me hath seen my Father also;" and, "The Word was God," for He was not made, inasmuch as "all things were made by Him;" and, "He thought it not robbery to be equal with God:" together with all the other passages of a similar order. But these statements have had a place given them, partly with a view to that administration of His assumption of human nature (administrationem suscepti hominis), in accordance with which it is said that "He emptied Himself:" not that that Wisdom was changed, since it is absolutely unchangeable; but that it was His will to make Himself known in such humble fashion to men. Partly then, I repeat, it is with a view to this administration that those things have been thus written which the heretics make the ground of their false allegations; and partly it was with a view to the consideration that the Son owes to the Father that which He is, —thereby also certainly owing this in particular to the Father, to wit, that He is equal to the same Father, or that

He is His Peer (eidem Patri æqualis aut par est), whereas the Father owes whatsoever He is to no one.

19. With respect to the Holy Spirit, however, there has not been as yet, on the part of learned and distinguished investigators of the Scriptures, a discussion of the subject full enough or careful enough to make it possible for us to obtain an intelligent conception of what also constitutes His special individuality (proprium): in virtue of which special individuality it comes to be the case that we cannot call Him either the Son or the Father, but only the Holy Spirit; excepting that they predicate Him to be the Gift of God, so that we may believe God not to give a gift inferior to Himself. At the same time they hold by this position, namely, to predicate the Holy Spirit neither as begotten, like the Son, of the Father; for Christ is the only one [so begotten]: nor as [begotten] of the Son, like a Grandson of the Supreme Father: while they do not affirm Him to owe that which He is to no one, but [admit Him to owe it] to the Father, of whom are all things; lest we should establish two Beginnings without beginning (ne duo constituamus principia isne principio), which would be an assertion at once most false and most absurd, and one proper not to the catholic faith, but to the error of certain heretics. Some, however, have gone so far as to believe that the communion of the Father and the Son, and (so to speak) their Godhead (deitatem), which the Greeks designate θεότης, is the Holy Spirit; so that, inasmuch as the Father is God and the Son God, the Godhead itself, in which they are united with each other, —to wit, the former by begetting the Son, and the latter by cleaving to the Father, —should [thereby] be constituted equal with Him by whom He is begotten. This Godhead, then, which they wish to be understood likewise as the love and charity subsisting between these two [Persons], the one toward the other, they affirm to have received the name of the Holy Spirit. And this opinion of theirs they support by many proofs drawn from the Scriptures; among which we might instance either the passage which says, "For the love of God is shed abroad in our hearts by the Holy Ghost, who has been given unto us,"

or many other proofs texts of a similar tenor: while they ground their position also upon the express fact that it is through the Holy Spirit that we are reconciled unto God; whence also, when He is called the Gift of God, they will have it that sufficient indication is offered of the love of God and the Holy Spirit being identical. For we are not reconciled unto Him except through that love in virtue of which we are also called sons: as we are no more "under fear, like servants," because "love, when it is made perfect, casted out fear;" and [as] "we have received the spirit of liberty, wherein we cry, Abba, Father." And inasmuch as, being reconciled and called back into friendship through love, we shall be able to become acquainted with all the secret things of God, for this reason it is said of the Holy Spirit that "He shall lead you into all truth." For the same reason also, that confidence in preaching the truth, with which the apostles were filled at His advent, is rightly ascribed to love; because diffidence also is assigned to fear, which the perfecting of love excludes. Thus, likewise, the same is called the Gift of God, because no one enjoys that which he knows, unless he also love it. To enjoy the Wisdom of God, however, implies nothing else than to cleave to the same in love (ei dilectione cohærere). Neither does anyone abide in that which he apprehends, but by love; and accordingly the Holy Spirit is called the Spirit of sanctity (Spiritus Sanctus), inasmuch as all things that are sanctioned (sanciuntur) are sanctioned with a view to their permanence, and there is no doubt that the term sanctity (sanctitatem) is derived from sanction (a sanciendo). Above all, however, that testimony is employed by the upholders of this opinion, where it is thus written, "That which is born of the flesh is flesh, and that which is born of the Spirit is spirit;" "for God is a Spirit." For here He speaks of our regeneration, which is not, according to Adam, of the flesh, but, according to Christ, of the Holy Spirit. Wherefore, if in this passage mention is made of the Holy Spirit, when it is said, "For God is a Spirit," they maintain that we must take note that it is not said, "for the Spirit is God," but, "for God is a Spirit;" so that the very Godhead of the Father and the

Son is in this passage called God, and that is the Holy Spirit. To this is added another testimony which the Apostle John offers, when he says, "For God is love." For here, in like manner, what he says is not, "Love is God," but, "God is love;" so that the very Godhead is taken to be love. And with respect to the circumstance that, in that enumeration of mutually connected objects which is given when it is said, "All things are yours, and ye are Christ's, and Christ is God's," as also, "The head of the woman is the man, the Head of the man is Christ, and the Head of Christ is God," there is no mention of the Holy Spirit; this they affirm to be but an application of the principle that, in general, the connection itself is not wont to be enumerated among the things which are connected with each other. Whence, also, those who read with closer attention appear to recognize the express Trinity likewise in that passage in which it is said, "For of Him, and through Him, and in Him, are all things." "Of Him," as if it meant, of that One who owes it to no one that He is: "through Him," as if the idea were, through a Mediator; "in Him," as if it were, in that One who holds together, that is, unites by connecting.

20. Those parties oppose this opinion who think that the said communion, which we call either Godhead, or Love, or Charity, is not a substance. Moreover, they require the Holy Spirit to be set forth to them according to substance; neither do they take it to have been otherwise impossible for the expression "God is Love" to have been used, unless love were a substance. In this, indeed, they are influenced by the wont of things of a bodily nature. For if two bodies are connected with each other in such wise as to be placed in juxtaposition one with the other, the connection itself is not a body: inasmuch as when these bodies which had been connected are separated, no such connection certainly is found [any more]; while, at the same time, it is not understood to have departed, as it were, and migrated, as is the case with those bodies themselves. But men like these should make their heart pure, so far as they can, in order that they may have power to see that in the substance of God there is not anything of such a nature as would imply that

therein substance is one thing, and that which is accident to substance (aliud quod accidat subsantiœ) another thing, and not substance; whereas whatsoever can be taken to be therein is substance. These things, however, can easily be spoken and believed; but seen, so as to reveal how they are in themselves, they absolutely cannot be, except by the pure heart. For which reason, whether the opinion in question be true, or something else be the case, the faith ought to be maintained unshaken, so that we should call the Father God, the Son God, the Holy Spirit God, and yet not affirm three Gods, but hold the said Trinity to be one God; and again, not affirm these [Persons] to be different in nature, but hold them to be of the same substance; and further uphold it, not as if the Father were sometime the Son, and sometime the Holy Spirit, but in such wise that the Father is always the Father, and the Son always the Son, and the Holy Spirit always the Holy Spirit. Neither should we make any affirmation on the subject of things unseen rashly, as if we had knowledge, but [only modestly] as believing. For these things cannot be seen except by the heart made pure; and [even] he who in this life sees them "in part," as it has been said, and "in an enigma," cannot secure it that the person to whom he speaks shall also see them, if he is hampered by impurities of heart. "Blessed," however, "are they of a pure heart, for they shall see God." This is the faith on the subject of God our Maker and Renewer.

21. But inasmuch as love is enjoined upon us, not only toward God, when it was said, "Thou shalt love the Lord thy God with all thy heart, and with all thy soul, and with all thy mind;" but also toward our neighbor, for "thou shalt love," says He, "thy neighbor as thyself;" and inasmuch, moreover, as the faith in question is less fruitful, if it does not comprehend a congregation and society of men, wherein brotherly charity may operate;—

Chapter 10. —Of the Catholic Church, the Remission of Sins, and the Resurrection of the Flesh.

—Inasmuch, I repeat, as this is the case, we believe

also in The Holy Church, [intending thereby] assuredly the Catholic. For both heretics and schismatics style their congregations churches. But heretics, in holding false opinions regarding God, do injury to the faith itself; while schismatics, on the other hand, in wicked separations break off from brotherly charity, although they may believe just what we believe. Wherefore neither do the heretics belong to the Church catholic, which loves God; nor do the schismatics form a part of the same, inasmuch as it loves the neighbor, and consequently readily forgives the neighbor's sins, because it prays that forgiveness may be extended to itself by Him who has reconciled us to Himself, doing away with all past things, and calling us to a new life. And until we reach the perfection of this new life, we cannot be without sins. Nevertheless it is a matter of consequence of what sort those sins may be.

22. Neither ought we only to treat of the difference between sins, but we ought most thoroughly to believe that those things in which we sin are in no way forgiven us, if we show ourselves severely unyielding in the matter of forgiving the sins of others. Thus, then, we believe also in The Remission of Sins.

23. And inasmuch as there are three things of which man consists, —namely, spirit, soul, and body, —which again are spoken of as two, because frequently the soul is named along with the spirit; for a certain rational portion of the same, of which beasts are devoid, is called spirit: the principal part in us is the spirit; next, the life whereby we are united with the body is called the soul; finally, the body itself, as it is visible, is the last part in us. This "whole creation" (creatura), however, "groaned and travailed until now." Nevertheless, He has given it the first-fruits of the Spirit, in that it has believed God, and is now of a good will. This spirit is also called the mind, regarding which an apostle speaks thus: "With the mind I serve the law of God." Which apostle likewise expresses himself thus in another passage: "For God is my witness, whom I serve in my spirit." Moreover, the soul, when as yet it lusts after carnal good things, is called the flesh. For a certain part thereof resists

the Spirit, not in virtue of nature, but in virtue of the custom of sins; whence it is said, "With the mind I serve the law of God, but with the flesh the law of sin." And this custom has been turned into a nature, according to mortal generation, by the sin of the first man. Consequently it is also written in this wise, "And we were sometime by nature the children of wrath," that is, of vengeance, through which it has come to pass that we serve the law of sin. The nature of the soul, however, is perfect when it is made subject to its own spirit, and when it follows that spirit as the same follows God. Therefore "the animal man receiveth not the things which are of the Spirit of God." But the soul is not so speedily subdued to the spirit unto good action, as is the spirit to God unto true faith and goodwill; but sometimes its impetus, whereby it moves downwards into things carnal and temporal, is more tardily bridled. But inasmuch as this same soul is also made pure, and receives the stability of its own nature, under the dominance of the spirit, which is the head for it, which head of the said soul has again its own head in Christ, we ought not to despair of the restoration of the body also to its own proper nature. But this certainly will not be effected so speedily as is the case with the soul; just as the soul too, is not restored so speedily as the spirit. Yet it will take place in the appropriate season, at the last trump, when "the dead shall rise uncorrupted, and we shall be changed." And accordingly we believe also in The Resurrection of the Flesh, to wit, not merely that that soul, which at present by reason of carnal affections is called the flesh, is restored; but that it shall be so likewise with this visible flesh, which is the flesh according to nature, the name of which has been received by the soul, not in virtue of nature, but in reference to carnal affections: this visible flesh, then, I say, which is the flesh properly so called, must without doubt be believed to be destined to rise again. For the Apostle Paul appears to point to this, as it were, with his finger, when he says, "This corruptible must put on incorruption." For when he says this, he, as it were, directs his finger toward it. Now it is that which is visible that admits of being pointed out with the finger; since the soul might also have been called corruptible, for it is itself corrupted by vices of manners. And when it is read, "and this mortal [must] put on immortality," the same visible flesh is signified, inasmuch as at it ever and anon the finger is thus as it were pointed. For the soul also may thus in like manner be called mortal, even as it is designated corruptible in reference to vices of manners. For assuredly it is "the death of the soul to apostatize from God;" which is its first sin in Paradise, as it is contained in the sacred writings.

24. Rise again, therefore, the body will, according to the Christian faith, which is incapable of deceiving. And if this appears incredible to anyone, [it is because] he looks simply to what the flesh is at present, while he fails to consider of what nature it shall be hereafter. For at that time of angelic change it will no more be flesh and blood, but only body. For when the apostle speaks of the flesh, he says, "There is one flesh of cattle, another of birds, another of fishes, another of creeping things: there are also both celestial bodies and terrestrial bodies." Now what he has said here is not "celestial flesh," but "both celestial bodies and terrestrial bodies." For all flesh is also body; but everybody is not also flesh. In the first instance, [for example, this holds good] in the case of those terrestrial bodies, inasmuch as wood is body, but not flesh. In the case of man, again, or in that of cattle, we have both body and flesh. In the case of celestial bodies, on the other hand, there is no flesh, but only those simple and lucent bodies which the apostle designates spiritual, while some call them ethereal. And consequently, when he says, "Flesh and blood shall not inherit the kingdom of God," that does not contradict the resurrection of the flesh; but the sentence predicates what will be the nature of that hereafter which at present is flesh and blood. And if anyone refuses to believe that the flesh is capable of being changed into the sort of nature thus indicated, he must be led on, step by step, to this faith. For if you require of him whether earth is capable of being changed into water, the nearness of the thing will make it not seem incredible to him. Again, if you inquire whether water is capable of being changed into air, he

replies that this also is not absurd, for the elements are near each other. And if, on the subject of the air, it is asked whether that can be changed into an ethereal, that is, a celestial body, the simple fact of the nearness at once convinces him of the possibility of the thing. But if, then, he concedes that through such gradations it is quite a possible thing that earth should be changed into an ethereal body, why does he refuse to believe, when that will of God, too, enters in addition, whereby a human body had power to walk upon the waters, that the same change is capable of being effected with the utmost rapidity, precisely in accordance with the saying, "in the twinkling of an eye," and without any such gradations, even as, according to common wont, smoke is changed into flame with marvelous quickness? For our flesh assuredly is of earth. But philosophers, on the ground of whose arguments opposition is for the most part offered to the resurrection of the flesh, so far as in these they assert that no terrene body can possibly exist in heaven, yet concede that any kind of body may be converted and changed into every [other] sort of body. And when this resurrection of the body has taken place, being set free then from the condition of time, we shall fully enjoy Eternal Life in ineffable love and steadfastness, without corruption. For "then shall be brought to pass the saying which is written, Death is swallowed up in victory. Where is, O death, thy sting? Where is, O death, thy contention?"

25. This is the faith which in few words is given in the Creed to Christian novices, to be held by them. And these few words are known to the faithful, to the end that in believing they may be made subject to God; that being made subject, they may rightly live; that in rightly living, they may make the heart pure; that with the heart made pure, they may understand that which they believe.

www.ingramcontent.com/pod-product-compliance
Ingram Content Group UK Ltd.
Pitfield, Milton Keynes, MK11 3LW, UK
UKHW020136250726
13967UKWH00002B/699

9 781643 730318